The Rise and Fall of the City of Mahagonny

The Rise
and Fall of
the City of
Mahagonny

BERTOLT BRECHT

TRANSLATED BY W.H. AUDEN
AND CHESTER KALLMAN

David R. Godine, Publisher Boston

First published in 1976 by
David R. Godine, Publisher
306 Dartmouth Street
Boston, Massachusetts
by arrangement with Suhrkamp Verlag, Frankfurt am Main.

ISBN 0-87923-149-1
LCC 75-11466

Printed in the United States of America

Frontispiece: Photograph of Bertolt Brecht by Gerda Goedhart.

The Rise and Fall of the City of Mahagonny

Introduction

The Rise and Fall of the City of Mahagonny must offend and repel its audience if it is to succeed. Bertolt Brecht's libretto and Kurt Weill's music cannot survive being made classic and safe. Riots greeted the first performances in 1930, and the opera's powerful negative example of a Paradise-city filled with victims makes just as vital an attack today. Specific corruptions and specific villainies don't matter: the problems themselves have not changed, only intensified.

The opera offers a lurid vision and a score which mingles lyric beauty with acrid cabaret tunes and simple ballads. Grotesque contrasts—love duets in a brothel and at an execution, drunken fantasies of escape leading straight to electrocution for poverty —convey the threat and demand action. Neither God, reduced to a parody playlet, nor chance, a hurricane which spares the foulest city in its path, will rescue society from itself. Modern capitalistic society destroys human choice and panders to the darkest and most cruel aspects of individual and community. *Mahagonny* charges its audience, members of that society, with self-cannibalism.

In both the score's eclecticism and the socially critical text, *Mahagonny* is far from alone in German and European music of the twenties and early thirties: the same collaborators' *Threepenny Opera*, of course, has had a continuous success. Yet that very success and *Threepenny Opera*'s link with the eighteenth-century *Beggar's Opera*, misunderstood by many audiences, finally make the modern work too easy to take, not offensive enough. Although less innovative and less well-known in the English-speaking world than *Threepenny Opera*, *Mahagonny* conveys its creators' vision more forcefully. The opera has been attacked for lacking realistic examples and an articulate social and political theory; moreover, Brecht's own political philosophy and his ideas about music in the epic theatre changed and became more definite after he wrote *Mahagonny*. Still, the opera can hardly be mistaken for anything but a harsh attack on many values and institutions of contemporary society. Brecht himself realized that the mechanism of opera production might temper his text's astringency; perhaps less clearly, he also saw a danger in the opera's assimilation into classic status. His response to these possibilities, and the consequent changes both Brecht and Weill made in *Mahagonny*, may be seen from the opera's early history.

OPERA—WITH INNOVATIONS!

In the spring of 1927, when Kurt Weill asked Bertolt Brecht to collaborate on a piece for the Baden-Baden Festival of Modern Music, an obvious choice was the so-called *Mahagonnygesänge*. Brecht had published these songs the previous year in *Taschen-postille* ('pocket breviary') and republished them in a nearly identical but larger edition entitled *Hauspostille* ('domestic breviary'). These verse songs require music, and *Hauspostille* contains some melodies for them, apparently composed by Brecht himself. With characteristic speed, the two men prepared the 'little' *Mahag-onny*, a one-act version containing five songs from *Hauspostille* and a new finale. They called their work a *Songspiel*, a typical play upon the old term *Singspiel* (that is, *opéra comique* or ballad opera) and presented it on July 17, 1927.

Although Brecht, working with Weill and Paul Hindemith, later brought other unconventional work before this prestigious festival, *Mahagonny* largely puzzled and offended the audience, even though that audience was temperamentally and intellectually among the most prepared to receive it with favor. Lotte Lenya has described the dismay when 'the stagehands began to set up a boxing ring on stage. The buzz increased as the singers, dressed as the worst hoodlums and frails, climbed through the ropes, a giant Casper Neher projection flashed on the screen hung behind the ring, and *Mahagonny* began—with a real, an unmistakable *tune!* The demonstration started as we were singing the last song . . . with the whole audience on its feet cheering and booing and whistling. . . . Later, I walked into the lobby of the fashionable hotel where most of the audience went for drinks after the performance, and found a frenzied discussion in progress. Suddenly I felt a slap on the back, accompanied by a booming laugh: "Is there no telephone?" It was Otto Klemperer. With that the whole room was singing the *Benares-song,* and I knew that the battle was won.'

Although Brecht and Weill prepared the little *Mahagonny* very quickly, its roots went far back in Brecht's career. 'Off to Mahagonny,' 'Who Lives in Mahagonny,' and 'God in Mahagonny' all come from before 1922, and the two most famous songs, the 'Alabama' and 'Benares' pieces, were written around 1925. Brecht even salvaged 'Lasst euch nicht verführen' from the unfinished play *Summer Symphony* (1919). This re-use of earlier material, as well as the constant revision of *Mahagonny* itself, well characterize Brecht's lifelong working patterns. Responses from the Baden-Baden Festival's artistic leaders, though neither entirely positive nor comprehending, nonetheless encouraged Brecht and Weill to use, in Brecht's words, 'theatrical music in accordance with a new point of view . . . the strict separation of the music from all the other elements of the entertainment.' The next year, this 'new point of view' reached a much larger public with *The Threepenny Opera,* a vastly successful Brecht-Weill collaboration and a descendant of the little *Mahagonny.*

Amidst the popular success and critical and political controversy which surrounded *Threepenny Opera,* Brecht and Weill continued to work on a much larger version of *Mahagonny.* It was finished more or less in April 1929, and published just prior to the first performance, on March 9, 1930, in Leipzig. The good burghers of Leipzig, expecting what Brecht called 'serious music [which] clings to lyricism and cultivates expression for its own sake,' were disappointed and outraged by what they saw and heard. Brecht's defenders, expecting another opportunity to advance their new and antitraditional views in defiance of the old ways, were not. Whistling, chanting, catcalls, and fist fights marked the battle lines of Brecht's and Weill's latest challenge to conventionality. Lotte Lenya, who played Jenny in the Berlin production, was in the audience that night: 'I have been told the square around the opera house was filled with Nazi Brown Shirts, carrying placards protesting the *Mahagonny* performance. . . . I was startled out of my absorption by the electric tension around us, something strange and ugly. As the opera swept toward its close, the demonstrations started, whistles and boos; by the time the last scene was reached, fist fights had broken out in the aisles, the theatre was a screaming mass of people; soon the riot had spread to the stage, panicky spectators were trying to claw their way out, and only the arrival of a large police force, finally, cleared the theatre.'

H. H. Stuckenschmidt, the distinguished German musicologist, reviewed the Leipzig production enthusiastically: 'If a way out of the present crisis in the realm of opera is to be found, the only hope lies in the quarter where Brecht and Weill are carrying out their ideological renovation of the traditional genres. . . . We have come to the point of decision: the decision that there must be a new form of opera, a radically different way for the theatre. . . . It is not the originality of the means which is decisive, but their power of suggestion. . . . The work forms a climax in the operatic history of the present age. For all its occasional beery humor, its adolescent romanticism, it strikes a powerful blow for the New Theatre, and for this very reason has aroused passionate hostilities. The whistling of the enemy partisans began even during the first act. Towards the end open tumult broke out. Brecher just managed to bring the performance to an end. And thereupon started a quarter of an hour of the most violent disputation, such as has not been heard for many, many years.'

Despite the controversies and compromises surrounding subsequent provincial performances in Kassel and Frankfurt, the Berlin opening (December 21, 1931) was to a degree an anticlimax, and the arguments, both for and against Brecht, which had greeted *Threepenny Opera* were predictably repeated. Even now, however, supposed commercial demands and timorous producers began to strangle Brecht's attempt to make a movie of *Threepenny Opera*, and the linked forces of artistic disagreement and increasing governmental opposition to Brecht's evident Marxism soon made further creative work almost impossible. Paul Hindemith, an important participant in the Baden-Baden Festival, had disagreed with Brecht over their joint work on the *Badener Lehrstück* (1929) and later joined other committee members in refusing *Die Massnahme* (1930) for the Berlin Festival which succeeded those at Baden-Baden. Even so great a play as *St. Joan of the Stockyards* (1929-1931) could not be produced. With the destruction of the Reichstag and the subsequent suppression of liberal and left-wing ideas and proponents, Brecht's extraordinary period of success—artistic, public, and scandalous—came to an end. Brecht and Weill both left Germany for an exile which lasted, in Brecht's case, fifteen years.

CULINARY OPERA AND CHEAP MUSIC

One of the dirtiest words in Brecht's lexicon is *kulinarisch* (culinary), typically applied to a work of art. The artist as cook, the art-work food, the audience as consumer: in their relation, nothing but unthinking pleasure and the satisfaction of a manufactured need by unreal means. For Brecht, traditional grand opera, or even the supposedly avant-garde opera of a Stravinsky, did not escape the twin evils of furthering pleasure and transforming itself into merchandise. Indeed, opera achieves all the wrong things even more completely than the traditional 'dramatic' theatre, for opera embraces the unreality of its means and demands that its audience respond irrationally. These views, along with an incisive description of *Mahagonny*'s innovative qualities, appear in Brecht's *Versuche* ('Essays' or 'Experiments') 2 (1930).

Brecht, writing with his friend and eventual publisher, Peter Suhrkamp, admits *Mahagonny* has many 'culinary' features; the big difference lies in *Mahagonny*'s attempt to 'bring the culinary principle under discussion,' or as he later said, 'The theme of the opera *Mahagonny* is the cooking process itself. . . .' This aim, and Brecht's personal symbolic system, help explain Jake Smith's death from overeating (scene 13): the wages of culinary art is death. As Brecht's later essay on music in the epic theatre shows, the central issue remains the relation between text and music; so long as the music and text attempt to 'work together' to form some single artistic entity, the opera will remain culinary. *Mahagonny*'s final form actually represents a step back towards orthodox opera and away from the clear division of music from text in *Threepenny Opera*. Only by separating the music and the text, by making them independent expressions of, or attitudes towards, the material can Brecht's goal be achieved. Music, like traditional dramatic practices, has 'stock narcotic attractions' which can be most effective when turned upon those usual practices, that is, when the process itself becomes the theme or when the audience's own preconceptions become the subject of dramatic scrutiny. Thus, in *Threepenny Opera*, 'the criminals showed, sometimes through the music itself, that their sensations, feelings and prejudices were the same as those of the average citizen and theatregoer.'

Weill's music for *Mahagonny* never wholly satisfied Brecht's demands, though he continued experimenting, especially in reducing the orchestra's size and making it a visible part of the stage machinery. As his remark on music's attractions suggests, the problem here—and with other, more obviously 'dramatic' features of his work—was showing up the stock responses as false and preventing the audience from accepting them immediately. In some ways, this goal might be more easily achieved in music than in other aspects because Weill could draw upon such traditionally taboo sources as jazz and cabaret music and popular song and thus defeat the audience's first impulse to irrational, culinary enjoyment. For the same purpose, Brecht deliberately uses the English word 'song' (in his theoretical writings and in *Songspiel*) to convey, as John Willett has pointed out, the opposite of what the Anglo-American tradition means by 'Lieder.'

A recent example illustrates the problems Brecht foresaw in opera production. Robert Craft attended the 1963 Hamburg production of *Mahagonny*, and in *Stravinsky: Chronicle of a Friendship, 1948-1971* he describes how 'risqué lines and situations are greeted with uncertain titters . . . the reception as a whole is exactly the opposite of the authors' intentions. The audience sits back and enjoys it as it would a musical or an operetta, albeit a strangely depressing example of either.

'After the performance, the scene in the restaurant of the Vier Jahreszeiten might be a continuation of the last scene of the opera. There the final abasement of society is represented by pickets with placards saying FUR GELD! while in the restaurant bellhops in floor-length aprons march about carrying the same kind of signs but summoning people to telephones: BITTE HERR STOLZ!' This production had certain problems not intrinsic to opera as a medium, but it also reveals the difficulty of uniting Brechtian methods and operatic practices. The audience's reaction would, to Brecht, confirm the need for the work's attack on present-day society.

During the period of his work on *Mahagonny*, Brecht had immersed himself in studying Marxist thought and continued to evolve theories of artistic utility. He argued that just as operatic music must cease to dominate or subserve the text and instead become an independent element of investigation, so too texts themselves must become reflective and deliberately invite argument and debate. From these developments came the so-called *Lehrstücke*, didactic plays for school, radio, or 'concert' performance on a bare stage. Brecht changed his plays' settings and organization, as well as the issues selected for study and the characters who present those issues. *Mahagonny*'s attack on the translation of human value into money, its mock trial, and the occasional debates also appear in Brecht's later plays, but the large share given to the music and the inexplicit social and politi-

cal theory make the opera more a summary of a period in
Brecht's career than an indication of his future work.

THE CITY OF NETS

Why 'Mahagonny'? Brecht loved coining names and words
which had half-references or multiple and contradictory references, such as Trinity Moses in this opera or Pierpont Mauler in
St. Joan of the Stockyards, or, for that matter, Mother Courage.
Arnolt Bronnen, Brecht's early friend and fellow playwright, has
twice ascribed the first use of 'Mahagonny' to Brecht's hatred of
Hitler's brown-shirted toughs, circa 1923; thus, the word carried
connotations of stupid violence, crudity, perhaps sensual indul-
gence. Hugo Schmidt has pointed out, however, that the word's
operatic version isn't pronounced the same way as the word for
mahogany wood (*Mahagoni* in German), which makes the brown
shirt/brown wood connection less distinct (though still plausibly
Brechtian). Probably the best explanation is none at all: H. O.
Münsterer remarks that Brecht simply liked the sound of the
word and its vague 'rich' connotations. Released from any
limited historical or strictly political context, 'mahagonny' re-
turns to Brecht's free manipulation, just as the setting itself
demands freedom from any 'logical' fact-ness or history.

More obviously pointed, the word *Netzestadt* ('city of nets' or
'snare-town') beautifully characterizes not only the founders'
goals but their disastrous self-entrapment as well. The opera's
indeterminately 'American' background shares many features
with Brecht's settings for other plays from this period; after
his turn to *Lehrstücke*, Oriental settings come into prominence.
Trying to establish Mahagonny's precise location is the response,
perhaps, of an audience which hopes to save itself from the
opera's most pungent attacks. *Mahagonny* takes place on some
American coast far from Alabama, somewhere between San
Francisco and Alaska but near Pensacola, when both motor
trucks and a gold rush coexisted. Weill, and to a lesser extent

Brecht, later sought to moderate the strictly 'American' background of the piece, apparently to emphasize its immediate German relevance. Thus the most recent printed score suggests some German names for the characters and carries a note (agreed upon by Brecht and Weill in 1930) urging producers to avoid Wild West and Cowboy allusions and references to a typical American milieu. Mahagonny is as international as the desire for money. For the same reasons, Weill (and the Berlin production) substituted a gallows for the electric chair; Brecht's *Versuche* text retained it.

Rather uneasily yoked with the almost continuous musical score, many Brechtian techniques appear in *Mahagonny*: banners and projections on a screen above the stage introduce and analyze the episodically arranged scenes; the action slips into articulate debates over a course of action, individual or collective; songs interrupt the more or less conversational dialogue. These features do not obscure the opera's clear organization and its clinical analysis of every Mahagonny. The first act establishes the city and concludes with its threatened destruction and Jimmy Gallagher's 'vision' of infinite freedom. The second act pursues that vision's effects, best shown by the repeated chorus:

> One means to eat all you are able;
> Two, to change your loves about;
> Three means the ring and gaming table;
> Four, to drink until you pass out.

Each of these 'do's' has its horrifying example: Jake Smith eats himself to death; Jimmy and Jenny have their tenuous love affair under Begbick's tutelage; Trinity Moses kills Alaskawolf Joe in a boxing contest on which everyone places bets; though penniless, Jimmy stands rounds for all. In the third act, Jimmy is electrocuted for lack of money, and the opera ends with Mahagonny's self-destruction.

Mahagonny's transformation from a 'suckerville' (Auden's neat translation) of oppressive and financially unsuccessful rules to a vast panorama of sensual pleasure which also collapses apparently represents for Brecht two faces of contemporary capitalistic society. It requires either (or both) a grinding obedience which produces empty 'pleasure' or an equally oppressive freedom based on the ability to pay. The hurricane which spares Mahagonny (and makes 'don't' into 'do it'), the moon, and memories of Alaska and the pure toil up north—all these fall before the uncomprehending rapacity of Mahagonny's managers and their clients. Whatever cannot be translated into money— the moon of Alabama or of Mahagonny (the chorus in scene 16), Jim's friendship for Alaskawolf Joe, love itself—all these have no meaning, no value, no effect in Mahagonny. Petty and ridiculous as the 'don'ts' were, the 'do's' manifest the single rule which underlay the original prohibitions (scene 18):

> . . . the penniless man
> Is the worst kind of criminal,
> Beyond both pity and pardon.

Neither God nor nature can destroy or reform Mahagonny. Only its own internal contradictions can do that. The placards carried in the closing procession summarize both those contradictions and the just demands which some of the characters have tried to articulate:

FOR THE NATURAL ORDER OF THINGS
FOR THE NATURAL DISORDER OF THINGS
FOR THE UNJUST DIVISION OF TEMPORAL GOODS
FOR THE JUST DIVISION OF SPIRITUAL GOODS
FOR PURE LOVE
FOR BRUTE STUPIDITY

and finally

FOR THE RE-ESTABLISHMENT OF THE GOLDEN AGE

Helpless before the oppression they have themselves helped create and from which they have occasionally profited, the people of Mahagonny offer this explanation for their city (scenes 1 and 22):

Why, though, did we need a Mahagonny?
Because this world is a foul one
With neither charity
Nor peace nor concord,
Because there's nothing
To build any trust upon.

The cities from which they come are as foul and sewer-ridden as
the city to which they flee. None of them and none of their
principles can 'do anything to help a dead man,' or a living one.

AUDEN AND BRECHT

Auden spent his first evening in Berlin at a performance of
Threepenny Opera, but his pleasure must have been more musical than literary, for as he later said, 'I knew no German and no
German literature.' Still, he learned quickly: Christopher Isherwood remembers that 'after two or three months in Berlin, he
began to write poems in German. Their style can best be imag-
ined by supposing that a German writer should attempt a son-
net-sequence in a mixture of Cockney and Tennysonian English,
without being able to command either idiom.'

In the Berlin of 1928, one could hardly miss Brecht—his
works, his fights, and the extraordinary talent of his associates.
Nonetheless, the two men seem not to have met. Just as
Hauspostille was part of Auden's Berlin reading, however,
Brecht certainly knew Auden's work around this time, since he
included both Auden and Isherwood in his projected 'Diderot
Society' or 'Society for Theatrical Research' as early as 1937.
Brecht's first temporary home after his exile from Berlin was
Denmark; from there he made several visits to New York, Paris,
London, and Moscow, in the first three of which he supervised
or observed productions of his work. Auden remembers first
meeting Brecht in Hollywood in 1941, but it seems hard to credit
that memory, since the two men would have had many earlier
opportunities to meet in London. Brecht certainly met Rupert

76-914

Doone, who had directed performances of Auden's and Isher-wood's plays at the Group Theatre. The most recent study of the Auden-Brecht link, by Margrit Hahnloser-Ingold, concludes that there is no definite evidence of a meeting before Brecht's departure for America.

Equally uncertain is the precise kinship, if it exists, between Auden's dramatic efforts and Brecht's. Some readers, empha-sizing the Marxism, or at least the anti-bourgeois feeling, and certain formal characteristics in Auden's plays, have speculated that Brecht influenced Auden's and Isherwood's joint work quite strongly. Both Auden and Isherwood have denied any conscious, direct connection. Auden's first play, *Paid on Both Sides* (1928), draws upon two traditions—the native English mummers play (or more generally, medieval drama) and Icelandic saga—which always fascinated him and continued to appear in his later work. Here there can be no question of specific influence, nor even of a more diffuse debt to German expressionism, since very little was available in English or on the English stage until the thirties, when Auden himself translated Toller. In subsequent plays, espe-cially *The Dog Beneath the Skin* (1935) and *The Ascent of F6* (1938), fantasy scenes reappear, but to label them 'expression-istic' or to go further and attach them to the German dramatic tradition which partly influenced Brecht himself would be an error. Auden has said: 'If there are aspects of the plays which remind the reader of German expressionistic drama, this is an accident—the real influence were [*sic*] the English Mystery or Miracle plays of the middle ages.' Breon Mitchell interviewed both Auden and Isherwood on the precise relation among their work, Brecht's plays, and the expressionistic tradition; he reports both writers' agreement that almost none existed, at least con-sciously. According to Mitchell, Auden's unpublished play *The Chase* (1934) provided much material for *The Dog Beneath the Skin* and reveals, again, many traditional English features. In addition to native origins, 'expressionistic' only to modern eyes, Auden mentioned Ibsen (*Peer Gynt*, but possibly also *Brand*) and Cocteau as 'influences.' 'Such German influence as there was,' Auden wrote, 'came from German Cabaret.' Given Auden's deep interest in music and especially opera, as well as his early innocence of German literature, this explanation sounds very convincing indeed. Isherwood remarks in *Exhumations*, 'If Auden had his way, he would turn every play into a cross between grand opera and high mass,' and Auden certainly remained extremely conscious of his duties to Weill's music when he came to translate *The Rise and Fall of the City of Mahagonny*.

Brecht, writing his 'Notes on the Folk Play' sometime in late 1940 (?), appears to regard Auden's and Isherwood's plays as independent developments: 'Their plays have something of the poetry of the old folk play but absolutely nothing of its naivety. They avoid its conventional situations and schematized characters.... Their situations are grotesque and at bottom they hardly have characters.... The linear story has been thrown on the scrap heap, the story itself as well as its line.... Their performance demands virtuosity... but it is the virtuosity of the cabaret.

'... Those plays which Auden wrote with Isherwood contain sections of great poetic beauty. He uses choruses and very fine poems, and the events themselves are sometimes elevated. It is all more or less symbolic, however; he even reintroduces allegory.... The poetry ought perhaps to be more in the actual situations instead of being expressed by the characters reacting to them.'

Auden's earliest direct creative contact with Brecht came in late 1943, when he joined Brecht and, for a time, H. R. Hays, in an adaptation of John Webster's Jacobean tragedy *The Duchess of Malfi*. This project, which eventually reached Broadway in 1946, went through a variety of complex vicissitudes, some of which are recorded in volume 7 of Bertolt Brecht's *Collected Plays* (1974). Auden's interest in the subject and love for Renaissance English literature finally led him to prepare his own adaptation of the play (copyrighted 1945; unpublished). Though the collaboration seems to have been happy, the results were not, largely because of external commercial and theatrical difficulties;

Brecht eventually withdrew his name from the adaptation and it appears nowhere in the New York publicity or reviews.

During his stay in America, Brecht seems to have become less enthusiastic about Auden and Isherwood, the latter of whom he saw quite frequently in Santa Monica. In his work-journal, Brecht groups Auden with Eliot and describes their poetry as 'augury,' rather humorless and ineffective as a spur to social change. By the war's end, Auden's political and religious beliefs had made him, too, much less a personal partisan of Brecht, though his admiration for the work, especially the poetry and the plays' songs, did not diminish. Even in the mid-1940's, Brecht was very anxious that Auden translate the songs for James and Tania Stern's translation of *The Caucasian Chalk Circle,* and he did. Later, Auden and Chester Kallman translated one of Brecht's exile-works, *The Seven Deadly Sins* (texts for a ballet first performed in Paris, June 7, 1933), just before beginning their work on *Mahagonny* in the summer of 1960. Still more recently, Auden translated the lyrics from *Mother Courage* for a 1966 production at the National Theatre in London. In Auden's commonplace book, *A Certain World* (1970), he includes 'Berthold Brecht (the lyric poet)' among 'those ... from whom I have learned most,' a view which his initial and continued admiration for *Hauspostille* confirms. That Auden drew a very sharp distinction between admiration for poet and poetry can be seen from an anecdote recorded by Robert Craft. The conversation, in January of 1966, turned to justifications for the death sentence, and Auden remarked: 'Well, there *have* been people on whom I can picture it being carried out. Brecht, for one. In fact, I can imagine doing it to him myself. It might even have been rather enjoyable, when the time came, to have been able to say to him, "Now, let's step outside." But of course I'd have given him a good "last meal." Still, you must admire the logic of a man who lives in a Communist country, takes out Austrian citizenship, does his banking in Switzerland, and, like a gambler hedging his bets, sends for the pastor at the end in the event there could be something in that, too.'

THE TRANSLATION OF *MAHAGONNY*

Auden's remark about the 'last meal,' however intended, augurs a certain uncongeniality between the poets when one turns to *Mahagonny*. Given Brecht's rigid separation of music from text and his hatred of 'culinary' aesthetics, the disagreement springs ready-made from Auden's *For the Time Being*: '. . . the real, the only test of the theatrical as of the gastronomic . . . [the Muse's] practice confidently wagers, is the mixed perfected brew.' Auden regarded *Mahagonny* as an opera above all and tailored his translation first to the music and then to the text itself. Describing his own libretti and others he had translated, Auden in 'The World of Opera' (published in *Secondary Worlds*) wrote: 'The verbal text of an opera is to be judged, not by the literary quality or lack of it which it may have when read, but by its success or failure in exciting the musical imagination of the composer. This does not mean that its literary quality is of no importance. Most composers will be more stimulated by good verses than silly ones.' His allegiance is clear. The problems of the original Brecht-Weill collaboration had similar origins; David Drew notes that 'Brecht had been persuaded somewhat against his will to embark on a libretto, and needed to be constantly reminded that musical considerations must come first.'

After the Berlin production of *Mahagonny*, in fact, the opera began to follow two separate courses, one charted by Brecht, the other by Weill. Versions of *Mahagonny* exist from different stages of each development. Auden and Kallman first published a partial translation (Act III) in *Delos* IV (1970), preceded by a note which implies that the translators considered the piano score's text as the main one.

Some characters' names have been changed to ease the translators' task: Jenny's last name is 'Jones' here, instead of Brecht's 'Smith' and Weill's 'Hill'; Jim Mahoney (in Weill's printed score) became Paul Ackermann in Brecht's *Versuche* and Jim Gallagher in the translation; similarly, Jack O'Brien became first Jakob Schmidt and then John Jacob Smith; Brecht gives translation's special strength is the way in which it captures the opera's shifts from vulgarity to lyricism without losing the force of ironic contrasts in both language and action. *Mahagonny* resists complacent responses, and the translators have enforced that resistance. Lust for money has not disappeared in a generation; societies and individuals still exploit humankind, offering grotesque substitutes for freedom. *Mahagonny* attacks such a society and, implicitly, demands its reformation. With the original's power undiminished, this translation offers new audiences the chance to experience that attack and reply to that demand.

A. R. Braunmuller

BIBLIOGRAPHICAL NOTE

Material on Brecht and his work increases almost daily. A few essential works in English (most drawn upon for this introduction) include: John Willett, transl. and ed., *Brecht on Theatre* (1964) and *The Theatre of Bertolt Brecht*, 2nd ed. (1961); Martin Esslin, *Brecht: The Man and His Work*, rev. ed. (1971); Eric Bentley, transl., Brecht, *Manual of Piety* (i.e., *Hauspostille*), with excellent notes by Hugo Schmidt (1966). Brecht's *Arbeitsjournal* has been published (1973) and an ancillary work, Klaus Völker's *Brecht Chronicle*, recently translated (1975). John Willett and Ralph Manheim are general editors of a major edition of Brecht's plays in translation, along with selected poems; four volumes have reached print to date. Eric Bentley and various British translators have published many texts, dramatic and poetic. Max Spalter has traced literary influences in *Brecht's Tradition* (1967); *Arnolt Bronnen Gibt zu Protokoll* (1954) and Bronnen's *Tage mit Bertolt Brecht* (1960) have much personal information, and H. O. Münsterer's *Bert Brecht: Erinnerungen aus den Jahren 1917-1922* (1963) is important for poems which later appear in *Mahagonny*. Two studies of Brecht's and Auden's literary relations have been mentioned: Breon Mitchell, 'W. H. Auden and Christopher Isherwood: The "German Influence," ' *Oxford German Studies* I (1966), and Margrit Hahnloser-Ingold, *Das Englische Theater und Bert Brecht* (1970). A thorough compilation is B. C. Bloomfield and E. Mendelson, *W. H. Auden: A Bibliography, 1924-1969*, 2nd ed. (1972); John Fuller has provided a helpful *Reader's Guide to W. H.*

Auden (1970). Christopher Isherwood's *Exhumations* has been quoted and his *Lions and Shadows* should be consulted on Auden's and his Berlin days.

The 1963 London production of *Mahagonny* occasioned a number of studies and reviews of which the most thorough are David Drew's pieces in *Musical Times* (January 1963) and *Opera* (February 1963). The portions of Stuckenschmidt's original review quoted here are from the latter; excerpts from Alfred Polgar's colorful review appear in Esslin's book. Stuckenschmidt has an interpretative essay in the pamphlet which accompanies the current Columbia (and Philips) recording of *Mahagonny*, from which Lotte Lenya's remarks have been quoted. Drew also edited the complete score published by Universal Editions, Vienna (1969), and there gives a very helpful account of the opera's diverse forms. General discussions of Weill's music and importance may be found in Theodore Adorno's and Stuckenschmidt's many works on modern music; John Willett devotes a section of his book to all Brecht's musical collaborators.

In addition to the information provided by these works, I have benefited from the generous personal assistance of Edward Mendelson and John Willett.

A. R. B.

NOTE

When Auden and Kallman published the third act of this translation
in the periodical *Delos* (in 1970), they preceded it with a brief note,
apparently shortened from a fuller version that referred to all three
acts, not merely the last. The portions of the note referring to the
first and second acts are lost. The version printed in *Delos* reads as
follows:

*This is a translation, not of a verse drama, but of an opera libretto:
the English versification conforms to the notes of Kurt Weill's music.
In some cases, this has involved changing the names of the characters. . . .*

*Some of the lines in 'Benares Song' are written in pidgin English
because Brecht believed that pidgin English was the lingua franca of
our age: this is extremely effective when it appears in the middle of
a German text, but when sung by characters to whom English is their
native tongue, it has no point.*

*Our version of the hero's farewell speech before electrocution is
based not on the text as printed in the piano score (Universal Editions,
Vienna), but on that which appears in the Suhrkamp edition of
Brecht's Collected Works (Versuche 1–4, Berlin, 1959).*

W.H.A.
C.K.

Act I

Why, though, do we need a Mahagonny?
Because this world is a foul one
With neither charity
Nor peace nor concord,
Because there's nothing
To build any trust upon.

The screen closes quickly and on it appears the title of

Two

WITHIN A FEW WEEKS A CITY HAD ARISEN AND
THE FIRST SHARKS AND HARPIES WERE MAKING
THEMSELVES AT HOME.

In front of this, JENNY *and six girls enter carrying large
valises. They sit on their valises and sing the Alabama Song.*

JENNY & GIRLS
Oh, show us the way
To the next whiskey-bar.
Oh, don't ask why!
For we must find the next whiskey-bar.
For if we don't find the next whiskey-bar
I tell you we must die!
Oh, Moon of Alabama
We now must say good-bye,
We've lost our good old mama
And must have whiskey
Oh, you know why.

Oh, show us the way to the next Mister Right
Oh, don't ask why, oh, don't ask why!
For we must find the next Mister Right
For if we don't find the next Mister Right
I tell you we must die!
Oh, Moon of Alabama
We now must say good-bye,
We've lost our good old mama

And must have misters
Oh, you know why!

Oh, show us the way to the next little dollar!
Oh, don't ask why, oh, don't ask why!
For we must find the next little dollar
For if we don't find the next little dollar
I tell you, we must die!
Oh, Moon of Alabama
We now must say good-bye,
We've lost our good old mama
And must have dollars
Oh, you know why.
They exit with their suitcases.

On the screen appears the title of

Three

NEWS OF THE FOUNDING OF A NEW JERUSALEM
REACHED THE BIG CITIES.

The screen opens. On the backcloth appears a projection showing a view of a metropolis and a photomontage of men's faces.

MEN *(offstage)*
We dwell in large dark cities: miles of sewers below them;
Thick over them, smoke; in them nothing at all.
No peace, no joy: here is no soil to grow them;
Here we quickly fade. More slowly they also shall fall.

FATTY *and* MOSES *enter with placards.*

FATTY
Far from the hullaballoo . . .

MOSES
(The big express-trains never bother us . . .)

FATTY

Lies our Joytown, Mahagonny . . .

MOSES

They just were asking where you've been so long . . .

FATTY

We live in an age that produces many city-dwellers city life
does not content: all are flocking to Mahagonny, the Joytown . . .

MOSES

Chips and chippies are cheaper!

FATTY

Here in all your cities there is so much noise,
So much ill-temper and discord
And nothing to build your trust upon.

MOSES

For yours is a foul world.

FATTY & MOSES

But once you puff with fellow
Mahagonny-dwellers
Smoke-rings white as snow,
Soon you'll feel your parchment yellow
Cheeks glow.
Sky-blue reflections turn
Gold in your drink:
Should San Francisco burn,
All there for which you yearn
Must, good or evil, churn
Down the same sink.

Here blue reflections turn
Gold in your drink:
Should San Francisco burn,
All there for which you yearn
Must, good or evil, churn
Down the same sink.

MEN (offstage)
> We dwell in large dark cities: miles of sewers below them;
> Thick over them, smoke; in them nothing at all.
> No peace, no joy: here is no soil to grow them;
> Here we quickly fade. More slowly they also shall fall.

FATTY
> Then off to Mahagonny!

MOSES
> They just were asking where you've been so long . . .

The screen closes. On it appears the title of

Four

THE NEXT FEW YEARS SAW THE DISCONTENTED
FROM EVERY COUNTRY MAKING THEIR WAY TO-
WARDS MAHAGONNY.

The title vanishes and JIM, JAKE, BILL *and* JOE *enter in front of the screen.*

JIM
> Off to Mahagonny

JAKE
> Where all the winds refresh,

BILL
> Where gin and whiskey rivers flow

JOE
> Past horse- and woman-flesh!

ALL FOUR
> Green and lovely
> Moon of Alabama,
> Shine for us!
> Underneath our shirts we've got

Money and we've got a lot!
That should smear some smile across
Your big and stupid face.

JIM

Off to Mahagonny
Where all the trade-winds blow,

JAKE

Where steaks are cut and blood runs out,
But no one runs the show!

ALL FOUR

Green and lovely
Moon of Alabama,
Shine for us!
Underneath our shirts we've got
Money and we've got a lot!
That should smear some smile across
Your big and stupid face.

JIM

Off to Mahagonny
Where all the winds refresh!

JAKE

Off to Mahagonny!

JOE

Off to Mahagonny
On swift and even keel,

BILL

Where civ-civ-il-i-zation
Will lose its scab and heal.

ALL FOUR

Green and lovely
Moon of Alabama,
Shine for us!
Underneath our shirts we've got
Money and we've got a lot!

That should smear some smile across
Your big and stupid face.
Exeunt.

On the screen appears the title of

Five

ONE DAY THERE CAME TO MAHAGONNY AMONG
OTHERS A MAN CALLED JIMMY GALLAGHER. WE
ARE GOING TO TELL YOU HIS STORY.

*The screen opens on a projection of a quay near Mahag-
onny.* JIM, JAKE, BILL *and* JOE *are standing before a signpost that reads:* TO MAHAGONNY. *A price-list hangs on the
signpost.*

JIM

When you arrive someplace the first time
You're a bit out of focus to begin with . . .

JAKE

You don't know where to go or how to go . . .

BILL

Who to order around . . .

JOE

Who to take off your hat to.

JIM

It's inconvenient
When you arrive someplace the first time.

BEGBICK *enters carrying a large notebook.*

BEGBICK

Gentlemen, welcome.
Just make yourselves comfy.
Consulting her notebook.

So you're the famous Jimmy Gallagher!
We hear tell of your knife tricks, Jimmy.
At your bedtime you must always have
English-made gin and bitters . . .

JIM

Pleased to meet you.

BEGBICK

Lady—short for Ladybird—Begbick.
They shake hands.
And for your arrival, John Jacob Smith,
We've put on our party clothes.

JAKE

Nice to know you.

BEGBICK

And you're known as Billy . . .

JIM *(introducing him)*
Bookkeeping Billy.

BEGBICK

Then you must be Joe.

JIM *(introducing him)*
Alaskawolf Joe.

BEGBICK

And just to show how glad we are to have you,
Prices will be cut till further notice.
She makes changes on the price-list.

BILL & JOE *(shaking hands with her)*
Thanks a million.

BEGBICK

Now you'll want to look into our latest crop of cuties . . .

MOSES *brings in pictures of the girls and sets them up. The
pictures are like the covers of old penny-dreadfuls.*

Gentlemen, every man carries an image of the ideal in his heart: one man's voluptuous is another man's skinny. The way this one can wriggle her hips should make her just about perfect for you, Joe.

JAKE

Maybe that one over there would suit me.

JOE

Actually, I had something a little darker in mind.

BEGBICK

What about you, Billy?

BILL

Me? I pass.

BEGBICK

And you, Jim?

JIM

No, pictures don't say nothing to me.
I have to pinch them and pat them to know
If it's really going to be love.
Come out, you beauties of Mahagonny!
We've got the dough, let's see your stuff.

JAKE, BILL & JOE

Seven years we worked Alaska:
That means frost-bite, that means dough.
Come out, you beauties of Mahagonny!
We like to pay for what we like.

JENNY & GIRLS (entering)

Here we are to help you melt Alaska:
Did you freeze there, but make the dough?

JIM

Well, hello, you beauties of Mahagonny!

JENNY & GIRLS

We are the cuties of Mahagonny:
By paying well, you'll get whatever you like.

BEGBICK (*pointing to* JENNY)
>That's the girl for you, John Jacob Smith:
>And if her behind doesn't have bounce in it,
>Your fifty dollars won't be worth their weight in toilet
>paper.

JAKE
>Thirty dollars . . .

BEGBICK (*to* JENNY, *shrugging her shoulders*)
>Thirty dollars?

JENNY
>Have you thought at all, John Jacob Smith,
>Have you thought what you can buy with thirty dollars
>now?
>Ten silk step-ins and no change.
>My home is Havana,
>From my mother I get my white blood.
>She often said to me
>'My lamb, don't sell yourself
>The way your mother used to
>For a buck or two.
>You can see what that life has done to her.'
>Have you thought of that, John Jacob Smith?
>Have you thought of that, John Jacob Smith?

JAKE
>For that, twenty dollars.

BEGBICK
>Thirty, sir. We don't bargain. Thirty.

JAKE
>Out of the question.

JIM
>Well, maybe I'll take her.
>You, what's your name?

JENNY

> Jenny Jones. Havana, Cuba.*
> I've been hereabouts for seven weeks now.
> I was down there in the larger cities.
> I'm game for all things that I am asked to do.†
>
> I know you Jimmies, Jimmies, Jimmies from Alaska well:
> You have it worse in winter than the dead have,
> But you get rich in hell.
> In leather jackets and your wallets stuffed with greenbacks,
> You come to see what Mahagonny has to sell.
>
> But this time's not like other Jims:
> They all went crazy for my limbs,
> Those limbs belong to you now, baby.
> It wasn't love before to me,
> So clasp your hand around my knee
> And drink from my glass too now, baby.

JIM

> Good. I'll take you.

JENNY

> Bottoms up, handsome.
>
> *But lots of people want to get away from Mahagonny; they
> enter in a rush, carrying their suitcases.*

JOE

> But who are these people?

PEOPLE

> Has the ship left?
> No, thank God! it's still at anchor!
> *They crowd off hurriedly to the quay.*

---

* *Or:* From Oklahoma.

† *Or (spoken):*

Jenny Jones. From Havana.
I got here just about nine weeks ago.
I used to live in the big cities down there.
I do anything that's asked of me.

BEGBICK *(shouting after them)*
  Bird-brains! Wool-heads! Look at them scuttling off to that
  ship like a pack of rats! And their pig-skin wallets are still
  fat with moola! Sons-of-bitches! Blue-nosed baboons!

JAKE
  I don't get it, why they're going.
  From a fun place, you don't run.
  Do you think that something stinks there?

BEGBICK
  You boys now, *you're* not going;
  You're coming along to Mahagonny.
  Call it a favor to me
  If you accept another cut in prices.
  She puts a new price-list up over the other.

JOE
  In this Mahagonny that we'd put so high a price on,
  Things are *too* cheap. That disturbs me.

BILL
  To me the place looks too expensive.

JAKE
  And you, Jimmy, do you think the place looks good?

JIM
  When we're there, it *will* be good.

JENNY & GIRLS
  I used to be so blue before,
  I never could be true before:
  It wasn't you before now, baby.

ALL
  We know these [They know us] Jimmies, Jimmies, Jimmies
  from Alaska well:

JENNY, BEGBICK & GIRLS
  They have it worse in winter than the dead have

JIM, JAKE, BILL & JOE

    But we got rich in hell.
    But we got rich in hell.

ALL

    In leather jackets and their [our] wallets stuffed with green-
    backs,
    They [We] come to see what Mahagonny has to sell.
    Exeunt for Mahagonny.

    *The screen closes. A projection appears of a street-map of
    Mahagonny.* JIM *and* JENNY *enter and walk up and down
    in front of this.*

Six

INSTRUCTIONS.

JENNY

    One thing I have learned when I meet a gent for the first
    time,
    That's to ask him what he is used to:
    Tell me then exactly how you would like me.

JIM

    As you are, you're exactly my type.
    If you would call me Jimmy
    I'd imagine you liked me a little.

JENNY

    Tell me, Jimmy, how you would like my hair done:
    Combed straight or with a wave?

JIM

    They both would look fine to me . . .
    Whatever's the mood you're in . . .

JENNY

    What are your feelings about underclothes, friend?

Should I wear step-ins when I'm dressed
Or a dress with nothing under?

JIM

Nothing under.

JENNY

As you like it, Jimmy.

JIM

But what would you like?

JENNY

Let's say it's much too soon for me to tell you.
Exeunt.

On the screen appears the title of

Seven

EVERY GREAT UNDERTAKING HAS ITS UPS AND
DOWNS.

*The screen opens. On the backcloth is a projection giving
statistics about crime and currency fluctuation in Mahagonny. Seven different price-lists. Inside the As-You-Like-
It Tavern,* FATTY *and* MOSES *are sitting at the bar.* BEGBICK
rushes in wearing white make-up.

BEGBICK

Fatty, we're ruined!
Moses, we're ruined! Haven't you noticed? People are leaving! They're rushing down to the quay with their bags. I
saw them there.

FATTY

What should keep them here—a sprinkling of bars and a
deluge of silence?

MOSES

And a fine lot of men they are! They hook a minnow and

they're happy; they puff smoke on the porch and they're satisfied.

ALL THREE

Our lovely Mahagonny
Has not brought in the business.

BEGBICK

Whiskey's down to twelve dollars a quart today.

FATTY

By tomorrow it's sure to drop to eight.

MOSES

And sure never to rise again!

ALL THREE

Our lovely Mahagonny
Has not brought in the business.

BEGBICK

I've lost all idea what to do. Everybody wants something from me and I've already given them everything. What more can I give to keep them from deserting us?

ALL THREE

Our lovely Mahagonny
Has not brought in the business.

BEGBICK

I, too, was once with a man who took me and put my
Back to the wall:
There we stood and talked for a while
And it was love that we spoke of.
Once all the money went
Talk like that lost its sexiness.

FATTY & MOSES

Ready money
Makes you sexy.

BEGBICK

It's nineteen years back!

It's nineteen years back that the misery of struggling for survival began, and it's sapped me dry. This was to be my last big scheme—Mahagonny, Suckerville. But the suckers refuse to get caught.

ALL THREE

Our lovely Mahagonny
Has not brought in the business.

BEGBICK

All that's left is to retreat quickly,
To follow our steps backwards through a thousand cities,
To travel in time backwards through nineteen years, boys.
Pack your luggage! Pack your luggage!
We've got to go back!

FATTY

Sure, Lady Begbick.
Sure, Lady Begbick, we'll go back. But it's *you* they're waiting for. *Reading from a newspaper:* 'In Pensacola yesterday the county sheriffs arrived in force and split to pick up Ladybird Begbick's trail. They made a systematic search of every house and rode off together . . .'

BEGBICK

God! Now nothing will save us!

FATTY & MOSES

Dear Lady Begbick,
It's a fact that crime has never paid well
And those dealing in vice do not
Live to grow old!

BEGBICK

With just a *few* dollars!
Yes, with just a few dollars
That we might have made in this enterprise
Planned as a snare, which wasn't a snare,
I could manage to hold the sheriffs off.
But weren't there some newcomers today?
They looked like money to me.
And maybe they'll spend it with us.

The screen closes. On appears the title of

Eight

SEEK AND YE SHALL NOT FIND.

The screen opens. The projection is of the quay near Mahagonny, as in No. 5. Coming away from Mahagonny, JIMMY enters followed by his friends who are trying to hold him back.

JAKE

Jimmy, what's the hurry?

JIM

What's there to keep me?

BILL

Why that look on your face?

JIM

I'm sick of seeing the word 'Forbidden.'

JOE

But the gin and whiskey are so cheap.

JIM

Too cheap.

BILL

And it's so peaceful here.

JIM

Too peaceful.

JAKE

When you feel like eating fish, you can catch one.

JIM

I don't like fishing.

JOE

You can smoke.

JIM
You can smoke.

BILL
You can sleep a bit.

JIM
You can sleep.

JAKE
You can go swimming.

JIM
You can go pick yourself a banana.

JOE
You can look at the water.

JIM *shrugs his shoulders.*

BILL
You can forget.

JIM
But it won't quite do.

JAKE, BILL & JOE
Beautiful are the sweet promises of nightfall
And gracious the long talks between friends beside the fire.

JIM
But they won't quite do.

JAKE, BILL & JOE
Soft and agreeable is the stillness
And enchanting is the concord.

JIM
But they won't quite do.

JAKE, BILL & JOE
Noble is the simple existence
And Nature's wonders are sublime beyond compare.

JIM

But they won't quite do.

I think I will eat my old felt hat,
The flavor, at least, will be new:
And why shouldn't a man eat his old felt hat
When he's nothing, when he's nothing, when he's nothing
else to do?

You've learned to mix your cocktails everyway,
You've seen the moonlight shining on the wall:
The bar is shut, the bar of Mandalay:
And why does nothing make sense at all?
You tell me, please, why nothing makes sense at all.

JAKE, BILL & JOE

Why, Jimmy, must you blow your top?
This *is* the bar of Mandalay.

JOE

Jimmy says he will eat his hat.

BILL

But why, why should you want to eat your hat?

JAKE, BILL & JOE

You mustn't eat your hat, Jimmy!
We *won't* let you do that, Jimmy!
Hat-eating goes too far—
Eating hats in a bar!
Shouting
We'll give you a beating,
Jimmy! Hat-eating
'S not what mankind was born for.

JIM

You tell me! What is it man was born for?

I think I will set out for Arkansas:
It may not be much, it's true.

But why shouldn't a man go to Arkansas
When he's nothing, when he's nothing, when he's nothing
else to do?

You've learned to mix your cocktails everyway,
You've seen the moonlight shining on the wall:
The bar is shut, the bar of Mandalay:
And why does nothing make sense at all?
You tell me, please, why nothing makes sense at all.

JAKE, BILL & JOE

Why, Jimmy, must you blow your top?
This *is* the bar of Mandalay.

JOE

Jimmy says he will eat his hat.

BILL

But why, why should you want to eat your hat?

JAKE, BILL & JOE

You mustn't eat your hat, Jimmy!
We *won't* let you do that, Jimmy!
Hat-eating goes too far—
Eating hats in a bar!
Shouting
We'll give you a beating,
Jimmy! Hat-eating
'S not what mankind was born for.

JIM

You tell me! What is it man was born for?

JOE

Well, now you've said your little piece, you can come along
with us like a good boy, home to Mahagonny.

They take JIM *back to Mahagonny.*

The projection changes to that for

Nine

Under a wide-open sky, in front of the As-You-Like-It Tavern, the Men of Mahagonny, including the four friends, are sitting on rocking chairs, smoking and drinking. They are listening to a piano, and dreamily watching a white cloud which travels back and forth across the sky. On the cloud printed notices replace each other each time it passes. The notices are:

KINDLY TAKE CARE OF MY FURNITURE. L.B.
WIPE YOUR SHOES BEFORE ENTERING. L.B.
DO NOT PUT YOUR FEET ON THE TABLE. L.B.
NO SPITTING. L.B.
ASHTRAYS HAVE BEEN PROVIDED: USE THEM. L.B.
DO NOT PICK YOUR TEETH IN PUBLIC. L.B.
DO NOT THROW RAZOR BLADES DOWN THE W.C. L.B.
PLEASE REFRAIN FROM USING INDECENT LANGUAGE AND
SINGING INDECENT SONGS. L.B.
KEEP THIS ESTABLISHMENT AS WE LİKE IT AND IT WILL
BE AS-YOU-LİKE-IT.

JAKE *(rapt, listening to the music)*
This is the *real* immortal Art!

JIM
Deep in the woods of ice-bound Alaska
Seven winters I toiled with three buddies together
Cutting down trees and hauling logs through the snow,
And I lived on raw meat and saved my earnings:
Seven years it's taken men to get me
Here where I now am.

There in a riverside hut for seven winters
Carving our curses with our knives in the table,
Talking of nothing but where we would go to,
Of just where we would go to when we'd saved enough
money,
Hungered, thirsted, sweated, shivered to
Get where we now are.

When our time was over, we picked up our earnings,
Out of all towns we had to choose from, we chose Ma-
hagonny,
Made our way here without stopping to rest
By the shortest route.
And what does it all add up to?
That no fouler place could exist
Nor any duller one be found on earth than
Here where we now are.

He jumps to his feet.

What's the big idea? You think you can treat *us* like that?
You've got a second think coming. Come out of there, you
As-You-Like-It slut! It's Jimmy Gallagher talking . . . from
Alaska . . . He doesn't like it here!

BEGBICK *(coming out of the Tavern)*

What don't you like here?

JIM

Your dungheap.

BEGBICK

I seem to keep hearing the word 'dungheap.' Did anyone by
chance say 'dungheap'?

JIM

You heard me. I said *Dungheap*.

The cloud shakes and goes quickly off.

JIM

Seven winters, seven winters hauling logs and cutting down
trees . . .

GIRLS, JAKE, BILL & JOE

He spent in cutting down trees . . .

JIM

And the river, and the river, and the river jammed with
floating ice . . .

GIRLS, JAKE, BILL & JOE

The river jammed with floating ice . . .

JIM

> Hungered, thirsted, sweated, shivered,
> Slaving like a beast to get here
> But I do not like it here for
> Nothing's going on.

JENNY & GIRLS

> Listen, Jimmy! Listen, Jimmy!
> Please be good and put that knife away.

JIM

> Hold me, hold me back!

JAKE, BILL & JOE

> Please be good and put that knife away.

JENNY & GIRLS

> Listen, Jimmy! Listen, Jimmy!
> Be a good boy, Jimmy, and behave.

JIM

> Hold me, hold me back!

JAKE, BILL & JOE

> Be a good boy, Jimmy, and behave.

JIM

> Seven years of felling timber,
> Seven years of cold and squalor,
> Seven years of bitter toil and
> This is all you have to offer:

BEGBICK, FATTY & MOSES

> You have quiet, concord, women.

JIM

> Quiet! Concord! Whiskey! Women!

JENNY, GIRLS, JAKE, BILL & JOE

> Put your knife back in your belt now!

MEN

> Qui-et! Qui-et!

BEGBICK, FATTY & MOSES

You can sleep here, smoke here, fish here, swim here.

JIM

Sleeping! Smoking! Fishing! Swimming!

JENNY, GIRLS, JAKE, BILL & JOE

Jimmy, put that knife away!
Jimmy, put that knife away!

MEN

Qui-et! Qui-et!

BEGBICK, FATTY & MOSES

We know these Jimmies from Alaska.
We know these Jimmies from Alaska.

JIM

Hold me, hold me back! Or there will be trouble.
Hold me, hold me back! Or there will be trouble.

JAKE, BILL & JOE

Hold him, hold him back! Or there will be trouble.
Hold him back! Hold him back! Hold him back!

JENNY & GIRLS

Hold him back! Hold him back! Hold him back!

MEN

We know these Jimmies from Alaska.
We know these Jimmies from Alaska.

BEGBICK, FATTY, MOSES & MEN

We know these Jimmies! We know these Jimmies!
We know these Jimmies, Jimmies, Jimmies from Alaska well:
They have it worse in winter than the dead have.

MEN

But you get rich in hell. But you get rich in hell.

JIM

Hold me, hold me back! Or there'll be trouble.

JENNY, GIRLS, JAKE, BILL & JOE

Jimmy, put your knife back in your belt now!
Please be good and put that knife away!
Come with us and be a gentleman.

JIM

Seven years of felling timber,
Seven years of cold and squalor,
Slaving like a beast to get where
Nothing's going on!

BEGBICK, FATTY & MOSES

Why can't stupid swine like these remain forever in Alaska?
All they ever want to do is spoil the fun of peace and concord. Throw the bastard out! He's had enough. Throw the
bastard out! He's had enough. Throw out the bum! Throw
out the bum! He's had enough.

JENNY, GIRLS, JAKE, BILL & JOE

Jimmy, please behave! Jimmy, please behave!
Jimmy, put your knife away!
Jimmy, put your knife back in your belt again.
Jimmy, be a gentleman.
Jimmy, don't make trouble with your knife!

JENNY

Hold him, hold him back!

MEN

Why can't stupid swine like them remain forever in Alaska?
All they ever want to do is spoil the fun of peace and
concord. That's the Jimmies from Alaska. That's the Jimmies from Alaska. Throw the bastard out! We've had
enough.

JIM

Hold me, hold me back! Hold me, hold me back!
Hold me, hold me back or there'll be trouble!
Hold me, hold me back or there'll be trouble!
For there's no life here!
For there's no life here!

He stands on a table.

No, not all your bars in Mahagonny
Will ever make a man happy:
There's too much charity
And too much concord
And there is too much
To build all his trust upon.

All the lights go out. Everyone remains as he is in the dark.

Ten

In enormous letters on the backcloth appears

TYPHOON!

and then

A HURRICANE THREATENS MAHAGONNY.

JENNY, GIRLS, FATTY, BEGBICK, MOSES & MEN
No! Not utter destruction!
Our golden Joytown will be lost!
For the raging storm hangs over the mountains:
We shall die, drown in the waters of death.
We face utter destruction,
A black, horrible end!

JENNY, FATTY & MOSES
O is there no wall to shelter me now?
O is there no cavern which will hide me?

GIRLS & MEN
O is there no wall to shelter us now?
O is there no cavern which will hide us?

JENNY, GIRLS, FATTY, BEGBICK, MOSES & MEN
We face utter destruction,
A black, horrible end!

We face utter destruction,
A black, horrible end!

The screen closes. On it appears the title of

Eleven

DURING THIS DREADFUL NIGHT AN UNTUTORED
LUMBERJACK CALLED JIMMY GALLAGHER HAD A
VISION IN WHICH THE LAWS OF HUMAN HAPPI-
NESS WERE REVEALED TO HIM.

> *The screen closes. The night of the hurricane. Sitting on the*
> *ground leaning against the wall are* JENNY, BEGBICK, JIM,
> JAKE, BILL *and* JOE. *All are in despair, but* JIM *is smiling.*
> *From backstage can be heard the voices of men in proces-*
> *sion as they pass behind the wall.*

MEN
> Stout be your hearts though dark be the night,
> Stand though the sun and the moon take to flight:
> Hence with idle wailing,
> Tears are unavailing;
> Face the fury of the storm and fight!

JENNY *(softly and sadly)*
> Oh, Moon of Alabama
> We now must say good-bye,
> We've lost our good old mama
> And must have whiskey, oh, you know why.
> *Repeat*

JAKE
> Why try to escape it?
> It's no use.
> To run away
> Cannot save you.
> The best thing we can do
> Is to sit here

And face it
Till the end comes.

MEN

Stout be your heart though dark be the night,
Stand though the sun and the moon take to flight:
Hence with idle wailing,
Tears are unavailing;
Face the fury of the storm and fight!

JIM *laughs.*

BEGBICK

What's the laugh for?

JIM

So, then—that's how it is!
Quiet and concord do not exist
But the big typhoons have existence.
So do earthquakes. You can ignore neither.
And the same is true of mankind:
It must destroy and bring ruin.
You're afraid of raging hurricanes?
You think that typhoons are shocking?
Wait till a man is out to have his fun.*

JAKE

Be quiet, Jim.

JOE

You talk too much.

BILL

Relax and smoke and forget.

MEN *(distant)*

Stout be your hearts though dark be the night.

JIM

You may build a tower taller than Everest:
Man will come and smash it to bits.

---

* *Or:* . . . is out for some amusement.

He'll do it for the hell of it.
The straightest way shall be made crooked
And the high place brought down to dust.
We need no raging hurricane,
We need no bolt from the blue:
There's no havoc which they might have done
That we cannot better, that we cannot better, that we cannot better do.

MEN (distant)

Stout be your hearts though dark be the night.

BEGBICK

Bad is the hurricane.
Even worse the typhoon.
But the worst of all is man.

JIM (to BEGBICK)

Listen! You've had placards put up
Upon which was written:
This is prohibited.
That you mustn't do.
That sort of thing spoils any happiness.
Boys! In that corner there is a placard.
It says there: *It is henceforth forbidden*
To sing any cheerful songs.
But before two o'clock strikes
You will hear Jimmy Gallagher
Singing a cheerful song
To show you that
It is *not* forbidden.

JOE

We need no raging hurricane,
We need no bolt from the blue;
There's no havoc which they might have done
That we cannot better do.

JENNY

Be quiet, Jim. You talk too much.
Come outside with me: make love to me.

JIM

    No. I've more to say.

    He comes to the front of the stage.

    If you see a thing
    You can only have for cash,
    Then fork out your cash:
    If someone is passing by who has cash,
    Knock him on the head and take all his cash:
    Yes, do it!

    If you fancy a lovely home
    Then enter a home
    And pick yourself a bed:
    If the housewife comes, make a twosome with her,
    If the roof begins leaking, get away!
    Yes, do it!

    If one morning a thought occurs
    New to your mind,
    Think that, like all thinking,
    It'll cost you cash and ruin your home:
    Think it, though! Think it, though!
    Yes, do it!

    For the sake of good order,
    The good of the town,
    For humanity's future
    And for your personal satisfaction,
    Do it!

    All have risen. They are now holding their heads high. JIM
    returns to them and they congratulate him.

MEN *(offstage)*

    Hence with idle wailing,
    Tears are unavailing;
    Face the fury of the storm and fight!

    BEGBICK *beckons* JIM *and goes into a corner with him.*

JIM

    From one life to a new life they departed

JENNY

    At equal speed with equal miles below them

BOTH

    And at each other's side alone we see them:

JENNY

    That so the crane and cloud may share the lovely,
    The lonely sky their passage heightens briefly;

JIM

    That neither one may tarry back nor either

JENNY

    Mark but the ceaseless lolling of the other
    Upon the wind that goads them imprecisely
    As on their bed of wind they lie more closely.

JIM

    What though the wind into the void should lead them
    While they live and let nothing yet divide them:

JENNY

    So for that while no harm can touch their haven,

JIM

    So for that while they may be from all places driven
    Where storms are lashing or the hunt beginning:

JENNY

    So on through sun and moon's only too similar shining,
    In one another lost, they find their power

JIM

    And fly from?

JENNY

                 Everyone.

JIM

                           And bound for where?

BEGBICK
>By itself, ready money
>Won't or can't make you sexy.

MEN (*without looking up*)
>By itself, ready money
>Won't or can't make you sexy.
>Ready cash cannot quite
>Make you sexy.

>*The room grows dark again.*

>Get to it soon,
>Get to it soon, *etc.*

>*The room grows light again. Another man enters, hangs his hat on the wall, and sits in the empty chair. The room slowly darkens again.*

>Mandalay won't glow
>Forever below
>Such a moon.
>Lovers, stop waiting.

>*An inner curtain is slowly drawn on the scene. Background music.*

>Your moon is setting . . .

>*When the stage grows light again,* JIM *and* JENNY *are seated on two chairs some distance from one another, in front of the inner curtain which now has* 'LOVING' *projected on it. He is smoking, she is putting on make-up.*

JENNY
>See there two cranes veer by one with another,

JIM
>The clouds they pierce have been their lot together

JENNY
>Since from their nest and by their lot escorted

LOVING.

in enormous letters is projected on the backcloth. On a platform, a bare room has been set up. In the middle of this room sits BEGBICK *with a girl seated on her left and a man on her right. Below the platform, and leaning their backs against it, the men of Mahagonny are sitting on a long bench. Background music.*

BEGBICK *(turning to the man next to her)*
Spit out your chewing-gum, boy.
See that your hands aren't dirty.
Give the girl time:
A short conversation's polite.

MEN *(without looking up)*
Spit out your chewing-gum, boys.
See that your hands aren't dirty.
Give the girl time:
A short conversation's polite.

The room slowly darkens.

Get to it soon,
Get to it soon,
Play that Mandalay immortal tune:
Love's not dependent on time for a lover.
Lovers, make haste,
Lovers, make haste,
Lovers, don't waste
What in seconds is over:
Mandalay won't glow
Forever below
Such a moon.
Lovers, stop waiting,
Lovers, stop waiting,
Hurry, the juicy moon
Is green and slowly setting.

The room has gradually grown light again. The man's chair is now empty. BEGBICK *turns to the girl.*

In the end I shall have rest.
To forget is sweet,
To forget is sweet.
More please! Give me more!
More please! Give me more!
More please! Give me more . . .
He topples over dead.

The men form a half-circle behind and remove their hats.

MEN

Smith lies dead in his glory,
Smith lies dead in his happiness,
Smith lies dead with a look on his face
Of insatiable craving,
For Smith went the whole hog
And Smith has fulfilled himself:
A man without fear,
A man without fear.

FIRST TENORS

Smith lies dead in his glory,
Smith lies dead in his glory.

SECOND TENORS

Smith went the whole hog:
A man without fear.
Smith went the whole hog:
A man without fear.

BASSES

Smith, Smith, Smith died in glory.

They put their hats on and come downstage.

Fourteen

MEN

Next we change our loves about.

The screen closes. When it reopens, the word

Thirteen

A YEAR LATER. MAHAGONNY IS BOOMING.

Men enter in front of the screen.

MEN

>One means to eat all you are able;
>Two, to change your loves about;
>Three means the ring and gaming table;
>Four, to drink until you pass out.
>Moreover, better get it clear
>That Don'ts are not permitted here.
>Moreover, better get it clear
>That Don'ts are not permitted here!

The men exeunt to behind the screen. The screen opens. On the backcloth in enormous letters is:

EATING.

A number of the men, including JIM, *are seated at tables laden with joints of meat.* JAKE *is seated at a center table eating incessantly. On each side of him a musician is playing.*

JAKE

>Two calves never made a man fatter:
>So serve me a third fatted calf.
>All is only half,
>All is only half:
>I wish it were me on my platter.

JIM

>Always, always insist on the whole,
>Never be content with half!

MEN

>Jake Smith! You're a stout soul!
>Eat away! Don't give up! One more calf!

JAKE

>Watch me! Watch me! Would you have guessed
>How much one person can eat?

Twelve

The curtain rises slowly; the screen is open. In a dim light, the men and girls of Mahagonny are waiting on a country road outside the city. As at the end of Act One, the projection on the backcloth shows an arrow moving slowly towards Mahagonny. Ever so often a loudspeaker makes announcements:

LOUDSPEAKER

The hurricane is now approaching Atsena at a speed of one hundred and twenty miles an hour. In Pensacola, eleven thousand are reported dead or missing.

The hurricane has reached Atsena. Atsena totally destroyed.

The hurricane is making straight for Mahagonny. It is now only three minutes away.

All are watching the arrow horrorstruck. Suddenly, a minute's distance from Mahagonny, the arrow stops. Dead silence. Then the arrow makes a rapid half-circle around Mahagonny and moves on.

The hurricane has veered in a circle around Mahagonny and is continuing on its course.

MEN & GIRLS

O wonderful salvation!
Our lovely city stands unharmed.
The raging hurricane veered away in a new direction
And pale death said to the waters: Go back.
Rejoice in our salvation!
Rejoice in our salvation!

The screen closes. Projection:

FROM NOW ON THE PHRASE *DO IT*, WHICH THEY HAD BEEN TAUGHT IN THAT NIGHT OF HORROR, BECAME THE MOTTO OF THE PEOPLE OF MAHAGONNY.

The projection goes off. In its place appears the title of

BEGBICK

So you think I was wrong to forbid anything.

JIM

Yes. Now I'm cheerful, I feel like tearing down all your precious notices. Even the walls will have to go. The hurricane won't pay you for them, but I will. Here. Take this.

BEGBICK *(to all)*

Let each one do just what he likes,
The storm will soon do it too:
So when a raging hurricane strikes
There's nothing we may not
There's nothing we may not
There's nothing we may not do.

JIM, JAKE, BILL & JOE

Clap your hands when a hurricane strikes:
Who cares for being immortal?
When a man can do just what he likes
Who's afraid of the storm at his portal?
Let it say
Any day:
Do you think you're immortal?

FATTY *and* MOSES *rush in excitedly.*

FATTY & MOSES

Destroyed is Pensacola!
Destroyed is Pensacola!
And the hurricane roars
On its raging way to Mahagonny!

BEGBICK *(exultantly)*

Pensacola!
Pensacola!
The sharp-eyed sheriffs are swallowed up,
The just alike with the unjust have been brought to nothing:
It must have taken them all!

JIM

You are free, I say, if you dare!

You may do all tonight that's prohibited.
Soon the hurricane will do it as well, so
Sing, as an example, for that's prohibited.

JENNY, BEGBICK, FATTY, MOSES, JIM, JAKE,
BILL & JOE
Come on, sing with us!
Come on, sing with us!
Come on, sing with us, sing any cheerful song,
If it's prohibited
Sing it with us!

MEN *(quite close behind the wall)*
Be quiet! Be quiet! Be quiet! Be quiet!

JIM *(jumping onto the wall)*
As you make your bed, so you lie on it,
The bed can be old or brand-new;
So if someone must kick, why, that's my part,
And another get kicked, that part's for you!

JENNY, BEGBICK, FATTY, MOSES, JIM, JAKE,
BILL & JOE
As you make your bed, so you lie on it,
The bed can be old or brand-new;
So if someone must kick, that is my part,
And another get kicked, that's for you!

*Lights out. On the backcloth is a map on which an arrow,
indicating the path of the hurricane, moves slowly toward
Mahagonny.*

MEN *(distant)*
Stout be your hearts though dark be the night!

SLOW CURTAIN

Act II

JENNY

For nowhere.

BOTH

So all true lovers are,
True lovers are, true lovers are.

JIM

Do you know what time
They have spent together?

JENNY

A short time.

JIM

And when they will veer asunder?

JENNY

Soon.

BOTH

So love to lovers keeps eternal noon.

The screen closes. The men enter in front of it.

MEN

One means to eat all you are able;
Two, to change your loves about;
Three means the ring and gaming table;
Four, to drink until you pass out.
Moreover, better get it clear
That Don'ts are not permitted here.
Moreover, better get it clear
That Don'ts are not permitted here!

The screen opens. The men go upstage. On the backcloth is now projected for

Fifteen

FIGHTING.

Under FATTY'S *supervision a boxing ring is being set up.*
On a platform to one side, a brass band is playing. JOE
enters with JIM *and* BILL.

JOE *(standing on a chair)*
> We have the honor today to present the greatest
> Fight ever: to be won by a straight Kayo—
> The famous bruiser, Trinity Moses,
> Versus me, the—Alaskawolf Joe.

FATTY
> What! You're challenging Trinity Moses!
> Boy! You'd best be making your will.
> That's no fight. It's murder. When that man
> Enters the ring, he's out to kill.

MEN
> What! Boy! Out to kill!

JOE
> That may be so, but the bid's worth making:
> All that I earned in Alaska I'm staking,
> For I believe that I shall win through.
> May all those who have known me longest
> Bet upon Joe to prove the strongest.
> Jimmy, I'm counting above all on you!
>
> All those who believe more in brains than in brawn,
> That Jack may be small but the giant is slow,
> Victory nearest when hope seems forlorn,
> Will lay their bets on Alaskawolf Joe.

JOE & MEN
> All those who believe more in brains than in brawn,
> That Jack may be small but the giant is slow,
> Victory nearest when hope seems forlorn,
> Will lay their bets upon Alaskawolf Joe!

JOE *has gone over to* BILL.

BILL
> Joe, we're close as friends, you know—

But it goes against the grain so
Chucking money down the drain, so . . .
I've put my money on Moses, Joe.

JOE *goes to* JIM.

JIM

Joe, my brother in work and in play
And my closest friend of any,
I am betting on you today
All I have, Joe, every penny.

JOE

Jim, when you say that, before me
Far Alaska rises up,
Those seven winters of bitter weather
When we felled timber, we two together.

JIM

Joe, my oldest friend, I tell you
All I prize I would give up:
Those seven winters of bitter weather
When we felled timber, we two together.

JOE

Jim, when you told me you'd dare it,
Our Alaska came in view:
The seven winters of bitter weather
When we felled timber, we two together.
You'll win your money, I swear it!
I'll do all a man can do!

JIM

Joe, I'd sooner lose, I swear it,
Than betray that life we knew:
The seven winters of bitter weather
When we felled timber, we two together.
Alaska I see and pair it
Ever, Joe, only with you!

The boxing ring is set up by now. MOSES *enters it.*

MEN

Give three cheers for Trinity Moses!
Good old Moses! Give him hell, man!

A WOMAN'S VOICE *(screaming)*

This is murder!

MOSES

I regret it.

MEN

Hit him so's he won't forget it!

REFEREE *(introducing the fighters)*

Our Trinity Moses, two hundred pounds.
Alaskawolf Joe, one-eighty . . .

MAN *(shouting)*

Coffee grounds!

Last preparations for the bout.

JIM *(from below)*

How you feeling?

JOE *(in the ring)*

All set.

JIM

Keep your end up.

JOE

You bet.

The fight begins.

MEN *(alternately)*

Let's go! Fight, boys! Shit! Quit stalling!
Now, Joe! No clinches! Foul! Get at it!
More blood! Neat one! Nail him! He's had it!
Watch it! Perfect! Hey! He's falling!

MEN *(together)*

Moses, keep slugging,

Make him swallow dirt!
Moses, beat him up, man!
Land them where they hurt!
Moses, land a left hook,
Now a right as well!
Sock him in the kidney!
Moses, give him hell!

JOE *drops to the canvas.*

REFEREE *(starts counting him out, then)*
The man's dead.
A burst of laughter from the men.

MEN *(dispersing)*
He couldn't take it.

REFEREE
The winner: Trinity Moses!

MOSES
I regret it. *Exit.*

MEN *(leaving)*
A Kayo's a Kayo . . .

BILL *(to* JIM: *they are alone in the ring together)*
I said he wouldn't make it.
I warned him he'd get it.
He has.

JIM *(softly)*
So long, Joe.

The screen closes. The men come before it.

MEN
One means to eat all you are able;
Two, to change your loves about;
Three means the ring and gaming table;
Four, to drink until you pass out.
Moreover, better get it clear
That Don'ts are not permitted here.

Moreover, better get it clear
That Don'ts are not permitted here!

The screen opens. The men go back upstage. On the back-cloth in enormous letters for

Sixteen

DRINKING.

The men sit down, put their feet up on the table and drink. Downstage JIM, BILL *and* JENNY *are playing billiards.*

JIM
Drinks on me. The gang is my guest.
I just want to show
That it's easy work at best
To be knocked out like Joe.
Lady Begbick, set them up for all the gents!

MEN
Good for Jimmy! It's a pleasure! It makes sense!

JIM, BILL, FATTY & MOSES
Mahagonny sure was swell,
Daily rates were twenty dollars;
Those who raised more special hell
Had to pay a little extra:
Then they all were steady callers
At Mahagonny's luxury saloon,
So they all lost their shirts and collars
But at least they saw the moon,
But at least they saw the moon,
But at least they saw the moon!
Both at sea and on land

JIM
Everyone who gets around is sure to get a skinning:
That's the reason everybody
Strips his own skin from his body

And when pelts are bought on every hand
With dollars, thinks he winning!

MEN (*shouting*)
Dollars!

JIM, BILL, FATTY & MOSES
Mahagonny sure was swell,
Daily rates were twenty dollars;
Those who raised more special hell
Had to pay a little extra:
Then they all were steady callers
At Mahagonny's luxury saloon,
So they all lost their shirts and collars
But at least they saw the moon,
But at least they saw the moon,
But at least they saw the moon!

JIM
Lady Begbick, set them up again for all the gents!

MEN
Good old Jimmy! Double whiskeys! No expense!

JIM, BILL, FATTY & MOSES
Both at sea and on land

BILL
Skins are up for sale and their consumption is extensive:
Who's to pay when everybody
Feeds the tiger in his body?
For those yellow pelts go cheaply and
The whiskey comes expensive!

MEN (*shouting*)
Whiskey!

JIM, BILL, FATTY & MOSES
Mahagonny sure was swell,
Daily rates were twenty dollars; *etc.*

BEGBICK
Time to settle the bill, gentlemen.

MEN

    Listen, listen, listen, listen,
    Hear how the wind in the rigging moans.
    Look now, look there, look now, look there,
    See where the heavens are pitch-black with menace!

BILL

    Shouldn't we lash ourselves to the mast if the violence of
    the storm increases?

JIM

    No, there is no menace, faithful shipmates,
    That's the black forest of Alaska.
    Disembark.
    We shall at last have peace.
    He climbs down and calls.
    Ahoy! Is that Alaska?

MOSES *(slipping over to him)*
    Come on, cough up the money!

JIM *(deeply disappointed)*
    No, it's Mahagonny.

    The men cluster around JIM, *raising their glasses.*

MEN

    Jimmy, old boy, you're a regular fellow
    Standing us the drinks that make us mellow,
    So with the same drinks we offer a toast:
    Long life to Jimmy, the perfect host!

BEGBICK

    Well, it's time for paying—pet!

JIM

    Look, Lady Begbick, but what can I do now
    If I'm not able to pay you yet?
    My money, I notice, all is through now.

BEGBICK

    What! you don't want to pay now?

JENNY

Jimmy, you must have a little more.
Why don't you go through your pockets again?

JIM

I was telling you before . . .

MOSES

What! the gentleman won't pay now?
What's that? No money? He *really* said it?
Do you realize what that means, my friend?

FATTY

Sweetheart, this is your unhappy end.

All except JENNY *and* BILL *have drawn away from* JIM.

BEGBICK *(to them)*

Couldn't *you* give him a little credit?

BILL *walks away without a word.*

And you, Jenny?

JENNY

Me?

BEGBICK

You. Why not?

JENNY

Don't make me laugh.
What will they ask a girl to do next?

BEGBICK

Wouldn't you even consider putting up half?

JENNY

No! If you have to have the precise text.

MOSES

Put them on!

JIM *is handcuffed. While he is also being tied,* JENNY *comes downstage and walks up and down during the following:*

JENNY

Let me tell you what my mother called me—
A bad word—yessir, that's what.
She swore I would end on a morgue-slab
Or an even more unhealthy spot.
Well, things like that don't cost much to say,
But what *I* say is: Wait around and see!
The talk doesn't matter two hoots
For you won't make those things happen to me!
We're human, not brutes.
As *you* make your bed, so you lie on it:
The proverb is old but it's true.
So if someone must kick, why, that's my part,
And another got kicked, that part's for you!
As *you* make your bed, so you lie on it
And no one will right what you do.
So if someone must kick, why, that's my part,
And another get kicked, that part's for you!

Have you heard yet what some guy told me?
'There's one thing can't be bought—
That's true love, the crown of existence.'
Also 'Give tomorrow no thought.'
Well, such things don't cost much to say
But what's mankind got to do with love
When each one gets older each day
And shorter grows the time we must make use of?
We're human, not brutes!
As *you* make your bed, so you lie on it:
The proverb is old but it's true.
So if someone must kick, why, that's my part,
And another get kicked, that part's for you.
As *you* make your bed, so you lie on it
And you buy the sheets for it too.
So if someone must kick, why, that's my part,
And another get kicked, that part's for you!

MOSES

You'll observe this miserable wreck
Who ordered drinks and couldn't pay his check.
Why, there's gall in that to choke one!

What man's viler than a broke one?
This is a capital offense!

JIM *is taken out.*

A thousand pardons for the disturbance, gents.

All take their places again, drinking and playing billiards.

MEN
Stay-at-homes do very well,
Don't need daily twenty dollars;
Those who also marry tell
How they save a little extra:
So today they all are callers
At the Lord-and-Shepherd's second-class saloon;
They keep clean there in shirts and collars
stamping in time with the music
But they never see the moon,
But they never see the moon,
But they never see the moon!
*They lean back slowly and put their feet up on the tables
again. Then, after a bit, they jump up, come downstage and
along the footlight and then go back to exit upstage.*
One means to eat all you are able;
Two, to change your loves about;
Three means the ring and gaming table;
Four, to drink until you pass out.
Moreover, better get it clear
That Don'ts are not permitted here!
offstage
Moreover, better get it clear
That Don'ts are not permitted here . . .

Seventeen

JIM *lies in the forest, one foot chained to a tree. Night.*

JIM
If the sky must lighten

Then a new goddam day begins.
But the sky still is covered up in darkness.
Let the dark, let the dark
Last forever,
Day must not, day must not
Break at all.

I'm still afraid they soon will be here.

I'll lie and sink in roots below me
When I hear them.
They'll have to tear my roots up with me
If they want me to go.
Let the dark, let the dark
Last forever,
Day must not, day must not break at all.

That's the kind of poker hand
They dealt you,
That's the hand you're stuck with,
That's the kind of poker hand
They dealt you,
Play it out.
Let the dark, let the dark last forever.
Day must not, day must not break at all!

What you lived of life
Was good enough for you,
What it brings now—
That's the hand you're stuck with.
Surely the sky won't ever lose its darkness.

It begins to grow light.

It must not lighten.
There must be no sunrise.
That means a new goddam day begins.

CURTAIN

Act III

Eighteen

EVERY CITY HAS ITS OWN NOTION OF WHAT IS
JUST, AND MAHAGONNY'S WAS NO SILLIER THAN
THAT OF ANY OTHER PLACE.

*The screen opens. A courtroom. In the center, a table and
three chairs. Behind them rise tiers of benches on which
the public is sitting, reading newspapers, chewing gum, and
smoking. The set suggests an operating theatre.* BEGBICK
is in the judge's chair, FATTY *in that of the defense at-
torney. On the prisoner's bench, to one side, sits* TOBY
HIGGINS. MOSES, *the prosecutor, is standing at the en-
trance.*

MOSES
Have the folks here all paid their admissions?
Three tickets still to go, at only five each!
Two absolutely first-rate tri-als:
Five dollars buys a seat for both!
Where could you find such a bargain?
A measly fin to watch Justice in Action!

*When no one else comes in, he resumes his place as prose-
cutor.*

First comes the case of Toby Higgins.

TOBY *rises.*

He is charged with premeditated murder
Done to test a newly purchased revolver.
Never yet
Has there been a crime so fraught
With brutal baseness.
Toby Higgins, you have outraged
Every decent feeling known.
Yea, the naked soul of sorely wounded Righteousness
Cries out for its retribution.
I therefore must now as prosecutor move
Owing to the stubborn unrepentance this defendant—
This abyss of mean obscene corruption—still displays,

That we let the Law take its course unhindered . . .
hesitating
And that he . . .
Under certain circumstances . . .
Be acquitted!

During the prosecutor's speech, a silent battle has taken place between BEGBICK *and the accused. By raising his finger,* TOBY *has indicated the amount of the bribe he is willing to pay. In the same manner,* BEGBICK *raises her demands higher and higher. The pause at the end of* MOSES' *speech marks the point where* TOBY *has raised his offer for the last time.*

BEGBICK
Has the defense any point to raise?

FATTY
Who's the injured party here?
Silence

BEGBICK
Since no injured party comes forward . . .

MEN *(spectators)*
Since dead men tell no tales . . .

BEGBICK
We by law have no course but acquitting him.

MEN
Since dead men tell no tales.

TOBY *goes to join the spectators.*

MOSES *(reading)*
Second, the case of Jimmy Gallagher
For seduction, negligence, subversion, and fraud.

JIM, *handcuffed, is brought in by* BILL.

JIM *(before he takes his place on the prisoner's bench)*
Billy, let me have a hundred dollars.
It may help to make the court more friendly.

BILL

    Jim, we're close as friends, you know:
    But with money, it's another matter.

JIM

    Bill, you can't have forgotten
    About our time up in Alaska:
    Those seven winters
    Of bitter weather
    When we felled timber,
    We two together.
    Please give me the dough.

BILL

    I have never forgotten
    About our time up in Alaska:
    Those seven winters
    Of bitter weather
    When we felled timber,
    We two together,
    And how hard we worked
    To make any money.
    That's why I simply can't
    Give you the money.

MOSES

    The accused ordered rounds of whiskey two times
    And broke a bar-rail, and did not pay.
    Never yet
    Has there been a crime so fraught
    With brutal baseness.
    Jimmy Gallagher, you've outraged
    Every decent feeling known.
    Yea, the naked soul of sorely wounded Righteousness
    Cries out for its retribution.
    I therefore must now as prosecutor move
    That we let the Law take its course unhindered.

During the prosecutor's speech, JIM *does not respond to* BEGBICK'S *finger-play.* BEGBICK, FATTY *and* MOSES *exchange significant glances.*

BEGBICK

Now we'll proceed to itemize the varied crimes
Charged to you, Jimmy Gallagher!
That, barely off the boat, you did with forethought
Seduce here a girl, by name Jenny Jones,
And made her do what you would
By means of your money.

FATTY

Who's the injured party here?

JENNY (*coming forward*)

Me. I am.

A murmur among the spectators.

BEGBICK

That, while we waited the big typhoon
You did, in that hour of desperation,
Persist in singing a cheerful song.

FATTY

Who's the injured party here?

MEN

The injured party has not come forth.
Maybe there's no injured party here.
If there's no injured party at all
Then there might be some hope for you, Jimmy Gallagher.

MOSES (*breaking in*)

But that very night, the man
Before you now behaved worse
Than a typhoon ever could,
Subverting all our city meant
By destroying concord and peace here!

MEN

Three cheers for Jimmy!

BILL (*standing up among the spectators*)

But this untutored lumberjack from Alaska
Had a vision of happiness that very night

And gave the laws of life to Mahagonny.
Remember, they came from Jimmy.

MEN

You must bring in acquittal then for Jimmy Gallagher
The lumberjack from Alaska!

BILL

Jim, I'm glad to do this for you
For I think of old Alaska,
Those seven winters
Of bitter weather
When we felled timber,
We two together.

JIM

Bill, what you've done here to help me
Takes me back once more to Alaska,
To seven winters
Of bitter weather
When we felled timber,
We two together.

MOSES (pounding the table)

And remember the boxing-match
When your dear 'untutored lumberjack from Alaska'—
To win mere money his motive—
Drove his best friend to sudden and certain death.

BILL (jumping up)

Yes, but who, august tribunal,
Who's the party whose punch really killed Joe?

BEGBICK

Well then, who did kill the so-called Alaskawolf Joe?

MOSES (after a pause)

That, Your Honour, is unknown to the court.

BILL

Of all those hanging around the ring that night,
Not one was risking a bet

On a man who might give his life there
But the man who stands before you risking his!

MEN *(alternately)*

The verdict must be guilty then for Jimmy Gallagher
You must bring in acquittal then for Jimmy Gallagher
The lumberjack from Alaska!

Applause and hissing.

MOSES

But now the crown of our charges comes:
Yourself, you ordered two rounds of whiskey
And destroyed one bar-rail just to amuse yourself—
Then tell me why, yes, why, Jimmy Gallagher,
You have failed to pay for consuming them.

JIM

Because I am broke.

MEN

The man is broke.
He consumes what he can't pay for.
Down, down, with Jimmy Gallagher!
Take him away.

BEGBICK, FATTY & MOSES

Who claim to be injured parties here?

BEGBICK, FATTY *and* MOSES *rise.*

MEN

Three injured parties have shown themselves.
They are the true injured parties then.

FATTY

Your verdict, august tribunal!

BEGBICK

Jimmy Gallagher, you are sentenced . . .

On the backcloth is projected the WANTED *poster that was seen at the opening of Act One.*

MOSES

For conniving at the murder of a friend ...

BEGBICK

To three days arrest.

MOSES

For destroying the concord and peace here ...

BEGBICK

A year's loss of civil rights.

MOSES

For the seduction of a girl by name of Jenny ...

BEGBICK

To four years in prison.

MOSES

For your singing forbidden songs during the big typhoon ...

BEGBICK

To ten years hard labor.
But for my two rounds of whiskey unpaid for,
And my one bar-rail as well unpaid for,
You by law must be sentenced to death in the electric
chair.

BEGBICK, FATTY & MOSES

For the penniless man
Is the worst kind of criminal,
Beyond both pity and pardon.
Wild applause.

The screen closes. On it appears for

Nineteen

AT THIS TIME A GOOD MANY PEOPLE IN MAHAG-
ONNY WHO WANTED SOMETHING DIFFERENT AND

BETTER BEGAN DREAMING OF THE CITY OF BEN-
ARES. BUT MEANWHILE BENARES WAS VISITED
BY AN EARTHQUAKE.

> JENNY, BEGBICK, FATTY, BILL, MOSES *and* TOBY *enter
> and seat themselves on high bar-stools and drink ice-water.
> The men read newspapers.*

BEGBICK
There is no whiskey in this town.

JENNY
No bar that doesn't get us down.

FATTY, BILL & MOSES

Oh!

BEGBICK *(sentimentally)*
Where is the telephone?

FATTY, BILL & MOSES

Oh!

JENNY *(urgently)*
Is there no telephone?

MOSES
Oh God, so help me, no.

FATTY, TOBY & BILL

Oh!

ALL
Let's go, let's go
To Benares where the sun is shining,
To Benares, Johnny, let us go.

BEGBICK
There is no money in this land.

JENNY
No boy that's glad to shake your hand.

BEGBICK
Where is the telephone?

JENNY

Is there no telephone?

MOSES

Oh God, so help me, no.

ALL

Let's go, let's go
To Benares where the sun is shining,
To Benares, Johnny, let us go.

BEGBICK

There is no prize here we can win.

JENNY

No door that lets us out or in.

FATTY, BILL & MOSES

Oh!

BEGBICK

Where is the telephone?

FATTY, BILL & MOSES

Oh!

JENNY

Is there no telephone?

MOSES

No, no, goddammit, no.

FATTY, TOBY & BILL

Oh!

They find out from the papers about the earthquake in Benares. They jump to their feet in horror.

ALL

Worst of all,
Benares is now reported perished in an earthquake!
O my dear Benares,
Now where shall we go? Oh!

JENNY

>Where can we go?

Exeunt. On the screen appears for

Twenty

EXECUTION OF JIMMY GALLAGHER. MANY OF YOU,
PERHAPS, WILL BE SHOCKED AT WHAT YOU ARE
ABOUT TO SEE. BUT, LADIES AND GENTLEMEN,
ASK YOURSELVES THIS QUESTION: 'WOULD *I* HAVE
PAID JIMMY GALLAGHER'S DEBTS?' WOULD YOU?
ARE YOU SURE?

>*The screen opens. On the backcloth is projected a general*
>*view of Mahagonny bathed in a peaceful light. Many peo-*
>*ple are standing about in groups. On the right, an electric*
>*chair is being erected.* JIM *enters accompanied by* MOSES,
>JENNY *and* BILL. *The men remove their hats.*

MOSES

>Good day!
>Didn't you hear me? I said 'Good day.'

JIM *(laconically)*

>Hi.

MOSES

>If you've any worldly business to wind up.
>You'd better do it now,
>For the gentlemen who are anxious to witness your de-
>parture
>Have no interest in your private affairs.

JIM

>Darling Jenny,
>My time has come.
>The days I have spent with you
>Have been happy days,

And happy too
Is the ending.

JENNY

Darling Jimmy,
I also have had my golden summertime
With you,
And I dread what
Will become of me now.

JIM

Jenny dear,
My sort are not so hard to find.

JENNY

That isn't true.
I know what is gone is gone forever.

JIM

Why, you're wearing a white dress.
Just like a widow.

JENNY

Yes. Your widow is what I am,
Jimmy, and I shan't forget you
When I'm just one of the girls again.

JIM

Kiss me, Jenny.

JENNY

Kiss me, Jimmy.

JIM

Don't forget me.

JENNY

Of course I won't.

JIM

Don't be sore at me.

JENNY

Why should I be?

JIM

Kiss me, Jenny.

JENNY

Kiss me, Jimmy.

JIM

And now I leave you, my dear,
To my best and last friend, Billy,
Who's the only one left
Of the four men who came
From the woods of cold Alaska.

BILL *(taking* JENNY *in his arms)*
So long, Jim.

JIM

So long, Bill.

*They turn towards the place of execution. A group of men
pass by singing.* JIM *stops and watches them.*

MEN

One means to eat all you are able;
Two, to change your loves about;
Three means the ring and gaming table;
Four, to drink until you pass out.

MOSES

Have you anything more to say?

JIM

Yes. At last I realize what a fool I've been. I came to this
city believing there was no happiness which money could
not procure. That belief has been my downfall. For now I
am about to die without ever having found the happiness
I looked for. The joy I bought was no joy; the freedom I
was sold was no freedom. I ate and remained unsatisfied;
I drank and became all the thirstier. I'm damned and so,
probably, are most of you. Give me a glass of water.

JIM *stands in front of the electric chair. During the following, he is being prepared for execution.*

Dreams have all one ending,
To wake and be coldly sure,
To see the dark descending,
To hear the wind portending
A night that shall endure.

JIM & MEN

Life, our only treasure,
Runs out before you know;
The deepest draught of pleasure
Will seem too short a measure
When you are told to go.

Daily we grow older,
We have but little time,
So leave the dead to molder:
Your hearts will soon be colder,
Your powers past their prime.

JIM, JENNY, MEN & GIRLS

Take not as your teacher
The tyrant or the slave,
And do not dread the preacher:
The end for every creature
Is nothing but the grave.

JIM

So you really mean to execute me?

BEGBICK

Why not? It's customary.

JIM

You don't seem to know that there's a God.

BEGBICK

A what?

JIM

A God.

BEGBICK

Oh, *Him!* Don't be silly. Didn't you ever see the play: *God*

Comes to Mahagonny? We'll put it on now for you, if you like; and you shall have the best seat in the house. Just sit yourself in this chair.

JIM *sits in the electric chair. The helmet is put over his head.*

MOSES
Ready.

MOSES *gives the signal to the executioner. Lights out. The screen closes.* JENNY, FATTY, BILL, MOSES *and a fourth man enter in front of the screen and play for the start of*

Twenty-one

'GOD COMES TO MAHAGONNY.'

FATTY, TOBY & BILL
One morning when the sky was gray
During the whiskey
God came to Mahagonny
God came to Mahagonny:
During the whiskey
We recognized God in Mahagonny.

MOSES, *who plays the role of God, detaches himself from the others, steps forward and covers his face with his hat.*

MOSES
Insatiable sponges,
Lapping up my harvest year by year!
Little have you reckoned with your Maker!
Are you ready now when I appear?

JENNY
Saw what they were, the people of Mahagonny:
YES answered the people of Mahagonny.

FATTY, TOBY & BILL
One morning when the sky was gray

During the whiskey
God came to Mahagonny
God came to Mahagonny:
During the whiskey
We recognized God in Mahagonny.

MOSES

Did you laugh on Friday evening?
I saw Mary Weeman swimming by
Like a salted cod-fish in the salt sea:
Mary never will again be dry.

JENNY

Saw what they were, the people of Mahagonny:
YES answered the people of Mahagonny.

FATTY, TOBY & BILL *(behaving as though they hadn't heard anything)*
One morning when the sky was gray
During the whiskey
God came to Mahagonny
God came to Mahagonny:
During the whiskey
We recognized God in Mahagonny.

MOSES

Whose is this ammunition?
Shot her, did you, shot my deaconess?
Are my thrones for brutes of your condition?
Is it drunken loafers I must bless?

JENNY

Saw what they were, the people of Mahagonny:
YES answered the people of Mahagonny.

FATTY, TOBY & BILL *(trying to distract Moses)*
One morning when the sky was gray
During the whiskey
God came to Mahagonny
God came to Mahagonny:
During the whiskey
We recognized God in Mahagonny.

MOSES

Down with all into hell-fire,
Stuff your Henry Clays into your pack!
Off with all of you to Hell, you scoundrels,
Wriggle in the Devil's crowded sack!

JENNY

Saw what they were, the people of Mahagonny:
NO answered the people of Mahagonny.

FATTY, TOBY & BILL

One morning when the sky was gray
During the whiskey
You came to Mahagonny,
You came to Mahagonny.
During the whiskey
Got going in Mahagonny.
But we won't budge a foot now!
We'll go on strike. We will never
Let you drag us off to Hell forever
For we *are* in Hell and always have been!

JENNY *(through a megaphone)*

Saw God, they did, the people of Mahagonny:
NO answered the people of Mahagonny.

JENNY, FATTY, TOBY & BILL

Saw God, they did, the people of Mahagonny:
NO answered the people of Mahagonny.

The stage darkens. Projection:

Twenty-two

IN THESE DAYS, BECAUSE OF THE UNHEARD-OF
RISE IN PRICES, GIGANTIC RIOTS BROKE OUT IN
MAHAGONNY, PRELUDING THE END OF SUCKER-
VILLE. THE RIOTERS CARRIED THE BODY OF JIMMY
GALLAGHER IN PROCESSION.

The screen opens. On the backcloth one sees Mahagonny in flames. BEGBICK, FATTY *and* MOSES *stand downstage. After they sing, groups of demonstrators enter in continual succession until the close.*

BEGBICK, FATTY & MOSES
Why, though, did we need a Mahagonny?
Because this world is a foul one
With neither charity
Nor peace nor concord,
Because there's nothing
To build any trust upon.

A GROUP OF MEN *(enter bearing Jim's hat and cane on velvet cushions)*
We need no raging hurricane,
We need no bolt from the blue:
There's no havoc which they might have done
That we cannot better do.

A SECOND GROUP *(enter with Jim's rings, watch, revolver and checkbook)*
As you make your bed, so you lie on it,
The bed can be old or brand-new:
So if someone must kick, that is my part,
And another get kicked, that part's for you.
As you make your bed so you lie on it
And you buy the sheets for it too.
So if someone must kick, that is my part,
And another get kicked, that's for you.

BEGBICK, FATTY & MOSES
Why, though, did we need a Mahagonny, *etc.*

JENNY & SOME GIRLS *(enter carrying Jim's shirt)*
Oh, Moon of Alabama
We now must say good-bye,
We've lost our good old mama
And must have dollars, oh, you know why.

BILL *enters at the head of another group of men.*

BILL

> You can bring vinegar—to him
> You can wipe his forehead—for him
> You can find surgical forceps
> You can pull the tongue from his gullet
> Can't do anything to help a dead man.

BILL'S GROUP

> Can't do anything to help a dead man.

> *Various placards are displayed. They run more or less:*

FOR THE NATURAL ORDER OF THINGS

FOR THE NATURAL DISORDER OF THINGS

FOR THE FREEDOM OF THE RICH

FOR THE FREEDOM OF ALL

FOR THE UNJUST DIVISION OF TEMPORAL GOODS

FOR THE JUST DIVISION OF SPIRITUAL GOODS

FOR PURE LOVE

FOR BRUTE STUPIDITY

> Can't do anything to help a dead man.

MOSES *enters at the head of a new group.*

MOSES

> You can talk good sense—to him
> You can bawl oaths—at him
> You can just leave him lying
> You can take care—of him
> Can't give orders, can't lay down any law to a dead man.

MOSES' & BILL'S GROUPS

> Can't do anything to help a dead man
> No one can do nothing for a dead man.

BEGBICK *enters with a third group that is carrying* JIM'S *body.*

BEGBICK

> You can put coins in his hand—for him
> You can dig a hole—by him
> You can stuff that hole—with him

You can heap a shovelful—on him
Can't do anything to help a dead man.

BILL, MOSES & THREE GROUPS OF MEN

Can't do anything to help a dead man
Can't do anything to help a dead man.

FATTY enters with a fourth group. They carry an enormous placard:

FOR THE RE-ESTABLISHMENT OF THE GOLDEN AGE

FATTY

You can talk about the glory of his heyday
You can also forget his days completely
You can change his old shirt for a clean one
Can't do anything to help a dead man.

ALL

No one can do nothing for a dead man:
Can't help him or you or me or no one.

CURTAIN

The text of this book was composed by Dix Typesetting in Linotype Palatino, a face designed by Hermann Zapf. Named after Giovanbattista Palatino, a writing master of Renaissance Italy, Palatino was the first of Zapf's typefaces to be introduced to America. The first designs for the face were made in 1948 and the fonts for the complete face were issued between 1950 and 1952. The paper is Risco Antique. The books were printed and bound by Halliday Lithograph Corporation.

Designed by Carol Goldenberg
Calligraphy by Stephen Harvard